Effortless Marketing Mastery: Strategies for the Modern Business

By

John Jesen

Copyright

About the Author

John Jesen is a seasoned marketing expert with years of experience in the ever-evolving landscape of digital marketing. Their expertise spans various industries, and they are known for simplifying complex marketing concepts into practical strategies. Through this book, the author shares insights, case studies, and actionable tips to help businesses navigate and succeed in the dynamic world of modern marketing.

INTRODUCTION

"Effortless Marketing Mastery: Strategies for the Modern Business" is a comprehensive guide that transcends traditional marketing paradigms, offering a fresh perspective on navigating the dynamic landscape of the contemporary business world. Authored by marketing expert Sarah Reynolds, this book serves as a beacon for entrepreneurs, business leaders, and marketing professionals seeking to revolutionize their approach to promoting products and services.

In the rapidly evolving realm of business, Reynolds unveils a roadmap that goes beyond conventional marketing wisdom. Drawing on her extensive experience and keen insights into consumer behavior, she introduces a nuanced understanding of the modern marketplace. The book contends that mastering marketing is not about amplifying effort but rather strategically aligning with the inherent dynamics of the digital age.

The introductory chapters lay the foundation by dissecting the changing dynamics of consumer behavior in the digital era. Reynolds explores the shift from traditional advertising channels to the omnipresent influence of social media, emphasizing the need for businesses to adapt and thrive in this interconnected landscape. Through illustrative case studies, she elucidates how successful brands have harnessed the power of social media, influencer marketing, and data-driven insights to create compelling narratives and foster genuine connections with their audience.

One of the key pillars of Reynolds' approach is the concept of authenticity in marketing. She argues that consumers today are not merely seeking products; they are searching for authentic stories and meaningful experiences. "Effortless Marketing Mastery" provides a blueprint for businesses to cultivate authenticity, encouraging them to showcase the human side of their brand, share behind-the-scenes glimpses, and engage in transparent communication. Reynolds asserts that authenticity builds trust, a currency more valuable than ever in the digital age.

The book also delves into the realm of content marketing, exploring how businesses can create compelling and shareable content that resonates with their target audience. Reynolds emphasizes the importance of storytelling and guides readers on crafting narratives that not only showcase their products or services but also tap into the emotions and aspirations of their audience. This strategic approach, she argues, leads to a more significant impact on brand recall and customer loyalty.

In the subsequent chapters, Reynolds explores the role of data and analytics in refining marketing strategies. Acknowledging the wealth of information available in the digital age, she demonstrates how businesses can leverage data to understand consumer preferences, track the effectiveness of campaigns, and make informed decisions. The book introduces practical tools and methodologies for implementing data-driven marketing, making it accessible even to those without a deep background in analytics.

A noteworthy aspect of "Effortless Marketing Mastery" is its emphasis on adaptability. Reynolds contends that in the fast-paced digital landscape, successful marketing strategies must be agile and responsive to changing trends. The book provides insights into monitoring industry shifts, staying ahead of the competition, and embracing innovation. Reynolds advocates for a mindset that views challenges as opportunities for growth, urging businesses to embrace change and continuously evolve their marketing approach.

Throughout the book, Reynolds weaves in real-world examples, showcasing how businesses of varying sizes and industries have successfully implemented the strategies outlined. From startups disrupting traditional markets to established brands reinventing their image, the case studies offer a diverse panorama of marketing excellence. These stories serve as both inspiration and practical illustrations, reinforcing the book's core principles.

In conclusion, "Effortless Marketing Mastery: Strategies for the Modern Business" is not merely a guide but a transformative manifesto for businesses seeking to thrive in the digital age. Sarah Reynolds provides a roadmap that transcends the complexities of modern marketing, making it accessible to novices while offering valuable insights to seasoned professionals. As a beacon for authenticity, adaptability, and data-driven decision-making, this book is poised to become an indispensable companion for those looking to master the art of marketing in the 21st century.

Chapter 1:Navigating the Marketing Landscape

In the dynamic realm of modern-day advertising, the shift to virtual strategies isn't just a desire; it is a need for agencies aiming to thrive inside the ever-evolving landscape. This bankruptcy takes a deep dive into the transformative adventure agencies adopt as they navigate the digital area, exploring the intricacies of key digital systems and their role in shaping powerful advertising and marketing strategies.

1. The Shift to Digital Strategies

The digital revolution has reshaped the manner businesses connect to their target audience. Traditional advertising and marketing channels, at the same time as still applicable, now share the degree with an array of digital opposite numbers. Social media, seo (SEO), e-mail advertising, and online advertising have ended up crucial additives of modern advertising strategies.

Social Media Dynamics:

Social media platforms have emerged as effective equipment for engagement and emblem visibility. Platforms like Instagram, Facebook, Twitter, and LinkedIn offer unique possibilities to hook up with diverse audiences. For instance, the rise of Instagram influencers has transformed the way brands reach and resonate with their goal demographic. Take the case of fashion brands collaborating with influencers to exhibit their merchandise authentically, mainly to increase brand recognition and purchaser trust.

SEO for Visibility:

Understanding the intricacies of seo is essential for corporations looking for visibility inside the vast digital landscape.

For example, take into account a small local commercial enterprise optimizing its internet site for local SEO. By incorporating place-precise key phrases and optimizing Google My Business profiles, such corporations beautify their possibilities of appearing in nearby seek outcomes, using foot traffic and increasing on-line visibility.

Data-Driven Decision Making

Digital marketing is inherently facts-pushed, relying on analytics and metrics for informed decision-making. Marketers music internet site visitors, consumer conduct, and social media engagement to advantage actual-time insights. An awesome instance is e-trade corporations making use of data analytics to apprehend consumer options, optimize product tips, and customize the web shopping revel in, in the long run boosting conversion prices.

2. Trends and Transformations

As era advances, marketing developments go through speedy differences. This phase explores contemporary tendencies shaping the digital advertising landscape, showcasing examples of agencies that have successfully embraced those tendencies to enhance their emblem presence.

Influencer Marketing Success

Influencer advertising and marketing exemplifies the electricity of authentic connections within the virtual age. Brands collaborate with influencers whose values align with their own, creating real endorsements that resonate with the audience. Take the instance of a splendor logo partnering with a makeup artist on YouTube. The influencer's genuine critiques and tutorials not only showcase the product but also construct trust among their fans, using sales and brand loyalty.

Immersive Experiences and Augmented Reality

Cutting-area technologies like augmented fact (AR) have redefined the manner brands interact with their target audience. Consider a fixtures retailer implementing AR functions on its cellular app. Customers can really surround furniture items of their homes earlier than creating a buy decision. This immersive experience does not best enhance consumer engagement however also reduces the probability of returns, contributing to a fantastic patron revel in. Staying attuned to those developments permits organizations to proactively position themselves for achievement in an ever-converting marketplace. By incorporating real-world examples, this chapter gives a comprehensive manual to navigating the digital advertising and marketing panorama, setting the stage for deeper exploration in subsequent chapters.

Chapter 1i: The Shift to Digital Strategies

In the dynamic panorama of modern-day marketing, the shift to digital strategies is not just a fashion; it's an essential transformation reshaping the manner corporations connect with their audience. This chapter delves into the intricacies of this transformative adventure, exploring key aspects of virtual advertising and imparting actual-world examples to demonstrate their effect.

1. The Digital Revolution

1.1. The Pervasiveness of Social Media

Social media platforms have emerged as the heartbeat of digital advertising, imparting unheard of opportunities for engagement and emblem visibility. Take the case of the iconic "Share a Coke " campaign through Coca-Cola. By personalizing their product with person names and inspiring customers to proportion their personalized cans on social media, Coca-Cola created a viral sensation, driving both online and offline engagement.

1.2. The Art and Science of search engine marketing.

Understanding the intricacies of Search Engine Optimization (search engine optimization) is vital for groups seeking prominence inside the virtual realm. Consider the instance of a startup inside the aggressive tech enterprise. By optimizing its internet site with applicable key phrases and creating first-rate content, the startup no longer best stepped forward its search engine scores but additionally hooked itself up as an authority in its area of interest, attracting natural traffic and capacity customers.

1.3. Data-Driven Decision Making

 In the virtual age, data is the foreign money of effective marketing. Analyzing consumer behavior, internet site site visitors, and campaign overall performance offers treasured insights for decision-making. For instance, an e-commerce giant employs records analytics to personalize product pointers based on man or woman user possibilities. This now not handiest enhances the patron revel in but also increases the probability of conversion, showcasing the electricity of records-driven techniques.

2. Social Media Dynamics

 2.1 Instagram: Visual Storytelling Instagram has advanced beyond a photo-sharing app to a powerful platform for visible storytelling. Brands like National Geographic leverage

Instagram's visual appeal to share fascinating testimonies. Through stunning imagery and compelling captions, they no longer handiest exhibit their logo ethos but additionally connect to a global target market, exemplifying the impact of visual content material inside the digital era.

2.2 Twitter: Real-Time Engagement

Twitter's actual-time nature makes it a unique channel for fast engagement. Consider the instance of a tech organization leveraging Twitter to provide real-time updates at some stage in product launches. By fostering direct conversation with their target market and addressing inquiries directly, the organization now not simplest builds logo loyalty however also creates a buzz around its products within the digital sphere.

3. Search engine marketing for Visibility

3.1 Local search engine marketing

For organizations with a neighborhood presence, optimizing for local seek is paramount. Imagine a small bakery imposing nearby search engine marketing techniques. By including location-unique keywords, preserving an updated Google My Business profile, and garnering fine reviews, the bakery will increase its visibility in local seek outcomes. This now not handiest draws close by clients however additionally strengthens the community connection, showcasing the tangible effect of localized SEO efforts.

3.2 Content Quality and Backlink

Building High-first-class content material is the cornerstone of effective search engine marketing. Consider the case of a software enterprise developing comprehensive publications and tutorials relevant to its enterprise. By continuously generating precious content material, the organization not best establishes authority inside the area but also attracts authoritative one-way links. This synergy of content material exceptional and backlink building contributes appreciably to improved search engine rankings.

4. Data-Driven Decision Making

4.1 Personalization in E-commerce

In the world of e-commerce, personalization is a recreation-changer. A retail large makes use of records analytics to research consumer purchase history and conduct. By enforcing personalized suggestions and targeted promotions, the enterprise complements the web purchasing experience. This information-pushed approach, now not the simplest, will increase patron pride but also drives repeat business, showcasing the strategic effect of leveraging statistics in e-commerce.

4.2 Performance Analytics for Campaign Optimization

For entrepreneurs, analyzing campaign performance is integral. Consider a virtual advertising enterprise walking a social media marketing campaign. By closely monitoring metrics together with click on-via fees, engagement, and conversion fees, the company identifies trends and areas for improvement. This iterative technique to campaign optimization ensures a better return on investment and illustrates the pivotal position of overall performance analytics in digital advertising and marketing success.

Conclusion The shift to digital strategies represents extra than a trade in tools; it signifies a paradigm shift in how organizations connect with their target audience. From the pervasive influence of social media to the precision of search engine marketing and the strategic use of records, corporations that embody these digital dynamics function themselves for success within the aggressive panorama of the digital age. As we navigate the digital advertising terrain, it's clear that holistic information of those techniques is important for crafting campaigns that resonate inside the ever-evolving virtual ecosystem.

Chapter 1ii: Trends and Transformations

In the dynamic landscape of virtual marketing, staying in advance requires not simply an information of present day strategies but additionally a eager awareness of emerging traits and alterations. This bankruptcy explores the ever-evolving nature of advertising tendencies, showcasing real-international examples of businesses that have efficiently embraced these shifts to elevate their brand presence and interact with their target market.

 1. Influencer Marketing: The Power of Authentic Connections

1.1 **Case Study**: Fashion Brand and Instagram Influencers Influencer marketing has emerged as a cornerstone of virtual techniques, illustrating the strength of authentic connections inside the digital age. Consider a fashion logo taking part with Instagram influencers. By aligning with influencers whose style resonates with the brand's identity, the business enterprise reaches a much wider audience with actual endorsements. The influencers, in flip, create content that authentically showcases the brand's products, fostering trust and loyalty among their fans.

1.2 Navigating the Micro-Influencer

Landscape Beyond macro-influencers, micro-influencers with smaller but pretty engaged audiences have gained prominence. A local espresso store, as an instance, may also associate with neighborhood influencers to show off its precise offerings. The authenticity and relatability of these influencers can create a more intimate reference to the network, mainly to expand foot site visitors and brand popularity.

2. Immersive Experiences and Augmented Reality (AR)

2.1 Case Study: Furniture Retailer's AR

Integration Immersive experiences, mainly the ones utilizing augmented fact, have converted how brands have interaction with their audience. Take the instance of a furniture store integrating AR functions into its cell app. Customers can simply place furniture gadgets in their houses earlier than making a buy choice. This does not best enhance the purchasing revel in however additionally reduces the uncertainty associated with online furniture purchases, ultimately boosting consumer pleasure and consideration.

2.2 Augmented Reality in Retail

In the retail quarter, augmented reality has been leveraged for virtual try-ons. A cosmetics brand, for instance, can provide an AR function that lets in clients to certainly attempt unique makeup merchandise before creating a purchase. This now does not best enhance the net shopping enjoyment however also reduces the probability of returns, showcasing the practical programs of AR in addressing client needs.

3. Video Content Dominance
3.1 YouTube and Educational Content

The dominance of video content material continues to grow, with structures like YouTube leading the way. Businesses are spotting the power of tutorial content to engage audiences. A software program corporation, for instance, may additionally create tutorial movies showcasing the functionality of its products. By offering treasured insights, the corporation not only educates its target market but also establishes itself as an authority in the industry, contributing to brand credibility.

3.2 Short-Form Videos and TikTok

Short-form video platforms like TikTok have redefined content introduction, especially among younger demographics. Brands have tapped into this fashion by using growing catchy and exciting short-form videos. Consider a garb logo launching a TikTok assignment wherein users show off creative approaches to style its merchandise. This no longer most effective fosters user-generated content material however also enhances brand visibility amongst a more youthful and fashion-savvy target audience.

4. Sustainability and Social Responsibility

4.1 Sustainable Practices in Fashion:
The growing emphasis on sustainability and social obligation has transformed consumer alternatives. In the style enterprise,

manufacturers adopting sustainable practices resonate nicely with eco-aware purchasers. A garb logo, as an example, may additionally spotlight its use of green substances and ethical manufacturing techniques. This not simplest attracts environmentally conscious clients however also contributes to a fantastic logo photo.

4.2 Transparency within the Food Industry: In the food enterprise, transparency concerning sourcing and production techniques has grown to be a key trend. An eating place, for instance, may additionally show off its commitment to locally sourced components and ethical farming practices. This transparency builds consideration with consumers who prioritize knowing the origins of the food they devour, illustrating the transformative effect of social obligation traits.

5. Rise of Interactive Content

5.1 Quizzes and Polls on Social Media

Interactive content has gained traction as an effective engagement device. Social media systems provide features like quizzes and polls that businesses can leverage. Consider a tech business enterprise the use of Instagram polls to collect comments on capacity product capabilities. This now not simplest engages the target market but additionally affords valuable insights for product development, showcasing the interactive abilities of social media.

5.2 Interactive Webinars and Virtual

In the generation of far off paintings and digital interactions, corporations are embracing interactive webinars and digital events. A commercial enterprise consulting corporation, as an instance, may additionally host a stay webinar where participants can ask questions and take part in polls. This no longer only enables real-time engagement but also positions the organization as a thought leader in its enterprise, demonstrating the transformative potential of interactive content material.

Conclusion

As advertising and marketing tendencies and alterations hold to shape the virtual panorama, companies that remain agile and embody innovation position themselves for sustained achievement. From influencer advertising and immersive reviews to video content material dominance and a commitment to sustainability, the evolving nature of those trends underscores the need for corporations to live attuned to the pulse of the market. By getting to know from real-international examples and adapting strategies to align with rising traits, corporations can navigate the

ever-converting marketing terrain with self
assurance and creativity.

Chapter 2: Understanding Your Audience

In the ever-evolving panorama of contemporary advertising and marketing, the bankruptcy on "Understanding Your Audience Quote" delves into the vital techniques that companies employ to realize and connect to their target demographic.

1. Building Personas for Precision

Creating designated purchaser personas serves as a foundational step inside the quest to understand the target market. These personas are complete representations that encapsulate diverse aspects, along with demographic statistics, behaviors, motivations, and pain points of the goal customers. The goal is to expand a nuanced knowledge of the people that make up the target audience, allowing for more unique and tailor-made advertising techniques.The art of personality creation involves a radical exploration of the ability patron base. It isn't merely about demographics but delves into the psychographic elements, shooting the attitudes, hobbies, and values that form purchaser conduct. For example, in the introduction of personas for a tech startup imparting software program answers, considerations may also extend past age and career to encompass elements such as technological proficiency, desired conversation channels, and attitudes closer to innovation.However, developing personas isn't a one-time undertaking. It includes a non-stop refinement procedure based totally on actual-time facts and evolving market traits. This dynamic technique guarantees that personas stay correct and reflective of the target market's converting choices. For instance, a retail emblem may also use real-time patron purchase records and engagement metrics to refine its personas continuously. By analyzing which merchandise resonates most with specific segments, the emblem can further tailor its offerings and marketing strategies, demonstrating the dynamic nature of audience information.

2. Embracing Market Segmentation

Market segmentation is a strategic method that includes dividing the audience into distinct corporations based totally on shared traits. These characteristics can span demographics, psychographics, or behavioral traits. The goal is to discover agencies with not unusual wishes and possibilities, allowing corporations to customize their advertising messages for optimum impact.Identifying segmentation variables is an essential initial step in this system. For instance, a travel organization may additionally choose to phase its target market primarily based on distinctive age corporations. By knowing the precise tour options and pursuits of millennials as opposed to baby boomers, the agency can tailor its advertising campaigns to attraction in particular to every section, optimizing relevance.This segmentation is not restrained to demographics on its own; it extends to behavioral patterns. For example, an e-trade platform may also phase its audience based on previous purchase history. By sending focused emails offering products associated with a consumer's past purchases, the platform complements the chance of repeat business. This personalized approach not only boosts engagement but additionally fosters a feel of connection among the emblem and the purchaser.

3. Psychological Insights into Consumer Behavior

Understanding the mental factors of customer conduct is a key issue of effective target audience engagement. Behavioral economics ideas, which explore the mental elements influencing decision-making, play a big role in shaping advertising techniques.Applying behavioral economics involves leveraging cognitive biases and heuristics. For instance, the principle of scarcity can be employed by means of highlighting constrained stock for a popular product, creating a feel of urgency that drives faster shopping choices primarily based on psychological triggers. Similarly, social proof, where people depend upon the actions of others as a guide for his or her very own conduct, may be harnessed thru testimonials and user-generated content material to construct credibility and trust.Establishing an emotional connection is some other effective approach in understanding and resonating with the target audience. This goes past the practical factors of a product or service and taps into the emotional blessings it is able to provide. For example, a well-being emblem may also consciousness at the emotional blessings of its products in addition to the functional elements. By aligning with clients' goals for well-being and self-care, the emblem is going beyond transactional relationships, developing a long-lasting emotional bond with its audience.

4. Adapting to Cultural Sensitivities

In an interconnected global, cultural information is paramount for corporations aiming to reach diverse audiences. Adapting advertising techniques to extraordinary cultural sensitivities ensures that the message resonates undoubtedly with each phase.Global businesses ought to navigate cultural competence in their marketing endeavors. This includes spotting and respecting cultural nuances, norms, and values. For instance, a multinational generation company tailoring its advertisements for diverse areas acknowledges the significance of knowledge and cultural differences. By doing so, the company guarantees that its message aligns with the cultural context, avoiding capability pitfalls and resonating undoubtedly with audiences global.For local companies, network engagement plays an important position in understanding their target market. Actively taking part in local events, helping network projects, and fostering authentic connections make a contribution to a deeper knowledge of the unique possibilities and values of the nearby target audience. For instance, a community bakery that actively engages in community events now not only is familiar with the specific tastes of its customers however also builds a loyal consumer base via proper connections.

5. Feedback Loops and Continuous Improvement

Establishing remarks loops is a crucial thing of ongoing target market expertise. Actively in search of consumer remarks thru surveys, reviews, and other channels gives valuable insights into client alternatives, pain points, and expectations. This continuous talk among the enterprise and its audience not simplest complements patron delight but additionally guides strategic selections.Leveraging customer feedback entails greater than simply collecting data; it calls for a dedication to non-stop development. For instance, an internet service platform may additionally continually are searching for customer remarks on its functions and functionalities. By reading these remarks, the platform identifies ache points and regions for improvement, permitting iterative improvements. This non-stop improvement cycle ensures that the platform remains aligned with evolving patron wishes and expectations.Adopting iterative techniques is vital for success in understanding the dynamic nature of target market possibilities. For instance, an e-studying platform may additionally constantly refine its content material based on person engagement metrics. By studying which topics resonate maximum with beginners, the platform optimizes its direction services to align with evolving educational needs. This iterative method guarantees relevance and sustained achievement in catering to the dynamic nature of target market alternatives.ConclusionUnderstanding the target audience isn't always a static undertaking; it's a dynamic technique that requires constant edition and a multifaceted technique. From developing certain personas and embracing market segmentation to tapping into psychological insights and adapting to cultural sensitivities, corporations have to navigate a complicated landscape to without a doubt connect to their target audience.By leveraging feedback loops and adopting iterative strategies, groups can't simplest realize the ever-changing panorama of target market alternatives however additionally respond with precision and authenticity. This information bureaucracy is the bedrock for success and enduring connections within the realm of current advertising. In essence, the adventure of understanding the target market is a continual exploration, one that shapes the strategies of businesses and guarantees their resonance with the evolving expectancies and needs of their target audience.

Chapter 2i: Building Personas for Precision

Building personas for precision is an important step in the strategic framework of information and connecting with a target market. In the realm of present day advertising and marketing, wherein personalization is an increasing number of valued, the advent of exact purchaser personas serves as a foundational strategy for groups in search of to tailor their approach to the unique needs and possibilities of their goal clients.

The Art of Persona Creation

Persona creation is a nuanced process that entails crafting fictional representations of ideal customers based totally on sizable research and insights. These personas encompass a big range of characteristics, consisting of demographics, behaviors, motivations, and pain factors. The objective is to increase comprehensive information of the individuals that make up the target audience, taking into account more particular and tailored advertising strategies. Consider a situation in which a tech startup is introducing a brand new software product. The advent of personas in this context might amplify past fundamental demographics together with age and task identity. It would delve into the psychographic factors, exploring elements like technological talent, favored conversation channels, and attitudes toward innovation. By knowing the intricacies in their capacity users, the startup can create advertising messages and product functions that resonate especially with each persona, ensuring a greater customized and effective approach. Persona creation isn't always a static manner; it includes non-stop refinement based totally on real-time facts and evolving market tendencies. As the virtual landscape and purchaser choices exchange, personas need to adapt to remain accurate and reflective of the target market's moving dynamics. For example, a retail logo would possibly use real-time consumer buy history and engagement metrics to continuously refine its personas. This iterative technique guarantees that advertising and marketing strategies live aligned with the evolving expectancies and behaviors of the audience.

Persona Refinement through Data

The refinement of personas is a dynamic technique that relies on insights derived from actual-time information. In the ever-changing panorama of customer behavior, groups should live attuned to shifts in alternatives and emerging developments. For instance, a retail brand's online platform might also make use of analytics to music person conduct and alternatives. By analyzing which products resonate maximum with unique segments, the emblem can further tailor its services and advertising strategies. This information-driven method guarantees that personas continue to be accurate and relevant, reflecting the present day wishes and expectancies of the audience. The process of personal refinement via information extends beyond quantitative metrics. Qualitative insights, inclusive of customer remarks and sentiment analysis, play a crucial function in understanding the nuanced factors of purchaser behavior. Combining quantitative and qualitative statistics permits organizations to color a greater holistic photograph in their target audience, permitting more accurate character creation and refinement.

The Dynamic Nature of Personas

Understanding that personas are dynamic entities is essential to their effectiveness. Consumer conduct evolves, encouraged with the aid of elements inclusive of technological improvements, societal modifications, and international events. Businesses should be agile in adjusting their personas to live ahead of these shifts. Consider a software corporation that gives project control answers. As far off work becomes greater popular, the personas created to start with can also want changes to reflect the converting desires and demanding situations of a distributed workforce. By staying attuned to those shifts and updating personas thus, businesses can make sure that their techniques continue to be aligned with the modern-day panorama.

Conclusion

Building personas for precision is a critical strategy for agencies aiming to connect with their target audience on a deeper degree. The art of personality creation entails crafting certain and multifaceted representations of best customers, considering a spectrum of traits from demographics to psychographics. Persona refinement is an ongoing system that is based on real-time facts and continuous models to evolving market developments. The dynamic nature of personas recognizes that client conduct is a problem to change, and businesses need to be proactive in adjusting their strategies to mirror those shifts.

In the ever-evolving international of modern marketing, wherein personalization and relevance are paramount, organizations that make investments time and effort in constructing and refining personas role themselves for fulfillment. By knowing the intricacies of their target market, they are able to craft messages and services that resonate authentically, fostering more potent connections and lengthy-time period customer loyalty.

Chapter 2ii: Embracing Market Segmentation

Embracing market segmentation is a strategic imperative for organizations seeking to tailor their advertising efforts to the diverse wishes and possibilities of their target audience. Market segmentation includes dividing the broader goal marketplace into distinct organizations based totally on shared characteristics, permitting agencies to craft more targeted and impactful advertising messages.

Identifying Segmentation Variables

The method of market segmentation starts off evolved with identifying the variables so one can be used to categorize the target market. These variables can span a range of things, together with demographics, psychographics, behavioral developments, and geographic region. For instance, a tour business enterprise might also pick out to phase its audience based totally on demographics, inclusive of age or profits stage. By know-how the precise travel options and hobbies of millennials versus baby boomers, the organization can tailor its advertising and marketing campaigns to appeal mainly to each segment. This centered approach guarantees that promotional efforts resonate extra effectively with the distinct characteristics of every group. In another example, an e-trade platform might also opt for behavioral segmentation, categorizing its target audience based totally on their usage patterns and buy records. By growing segments of frequent shoppers, occasional buyers, and first-time visitors, the platform can deploy personalized advertising messages to every organization. This no longer best complements the relevance of the communication but additionally fosters a experience of connection between the emblem and the client.

Personalization in Email Marketing

One of the tangible effects of embracing market segmentation is the potential to put in force personalized conversation strategies, in particular in e mail advertising and marketing. Segmentation permits groups to craft e-mail campaigns which might be tailored to the particular options and behaviors of various target market segments. For instance, an e-commerce platform can send targeted emails proposing products related to a customer's beyond purchases. This no longer most effectively increases the likelihood of repeat enterprise but also enhances customer engagement. By informing the precise pursuits and preferences of every phase, companies can deliver content material that is more likely to capture the eye and interest of the recipient.

Geographic Segmentation for Local Relevance

Geographic segmentation is any other powerful approach, particularly for groups with a physical presence in precise areas. This segmentation permits businesses to conform their advertising and marketing strategies to the particular traits and choices of various locales. Consider a multinational restaurant chain. By embracing geographic segmentation, the chain can tailor its menu services to align with nearby tastes and possibilities. This guarantees that every eating place location caters to the specific culinary expectations of its network, improving neighborhood relevance and patron satisfaction.

Customizing Product Offerings

Market segmentation now not best affects advertising messages but also shapes product offerings. Businesses can customize their products to meet the wonderful wishes and possibilities of various segments inside their target market. For example, a tech organization may additionally provide versions of a product to cater to special segments based totally on their technical skills ability. An extra advanced model of software could be focused toward tech-savvy customers, while a simplified version is probably tailor-made for individuals who prefer a person-pleasant experience. This customization guarantees that the product aligns with the various stages of know-how inside the audience.

The Role of Data in Segmentation

The successful implementation of marketplace segmentation is based heavily on records analytics. Businesses leverage records to identify patterns, traits, and traits inside their target market, taking into consideration extra correct segmentation. For instance, an online retail platform may also use information analytics to song user behavior, inclusive of browsing records, seek queries, and purchase patterns. By analyzing this information, the platform can pick out commonalities within one-of-a-kind user segments and create personalized purchasing reviews. This statistics-pushed method guarantees that segmentation is not entirely based on assumptions however is grounded in actual-time insights.

Challenges and Considerations

While marketplace segmentation offers several blessings, it isn't without demanding situations. Businesses need to navigate the delicate stability among developing meaningful segments and heading off oversimplification. Overly extensive   can also omit nuances inside the target market, whilst overly granular segmentation can lead to advertising inefficiencies. Additionally, corporations need to be mindful of ability biases in their records, as skewed or incomplete data can lead to inaccurate segmentation. Regularly validating and updating segmentation standards primarily based on clean information enables certain accuracy and relevance.

Conclusion Embracing marketplace segmentation is a strategic vital for groups aiming to navigate the complexities of the contemporary market. By figuring out segmentation variables, organizations can categorize their target audience into awesome groups based on shared characteristics, allowing greater targeted and customized advertising efforts. The practical effects of segmentation are glaring in customized email marketing, geographic relevance, customized product services, and information-driven decision-making. Through segmentation, groups can optimize their assets, improve client engagement, and beautify typical advertising effectiveness. While demanding situations exist, thoughtful consideration of segmentation variables, reliance on accurate information, and a dedication to ongoing refinement can help groups harness the electricity of market segmentation effectively. In the dynamic panorama of current advertising, in which personalization and relevance are paramount, groups that include segmentation role themselves to forge more potent connections with their numerous audience, in the long run driving achievement in an aggressive market.

Chapter 3: Digital Platform Mastery

Mastering virtual platforms is an essential component of thriving in cutting-edge business landscapes. Digital structures embody numerous online spaces, from social media networks like Facebook and Instagram to e-commerce systems which include Amazon and Shopify. They offer organizations with exceptional possibilities to connect to their target audience, enlarge their reach, and build a sturdy online presence.

1.Navigating the Digital Landscape

Understanding the particular dynamics of each platform is crucial. Social media structures have distinct vibes – Facebook for connecting with pals, Instagram for visuals, Twitter for actual-time updates, and LinkedIn for expert networking. Tailoring content material to suit the essence of every platform ensures that agencies efficiently interact with their target audience.

2. E-trade Excellence

In the world of e-commerce, structures like Shopify and Amazon revolutionize the way products and services are bought and bought. Mastering e-commerce involves optimizing product listings, making sure an unbroken buying revels in, and leveraging analytics to understand client conduct. Businesses can streamline transactions, reach an international audience, and maximize their online income ability.

3.Content Distribution Strategies

Content creation is essential, however understanding where and the way to share it is equally important. Different platforms cater to distinctive content sorts. LinkedIn may be appropriate for expert articles, even as Pinterest flourishes on visually rich content material. Understanding these nuances guarantees that groups maximize the effect in their content distribution efforts.

4.Leveraging Data and Analytics

Making informed decisions inside the virtual realm includes leveraging the records generated by digital structures. Insights into personal behavior, alternatives, and traits permit businesses to optimize strategies, improve customer reviews, and stay ahead of market tendencies. Analyzing key metrics such as internet site site visitors, engagement prices, and conversion charges gauges the effectiveness of virtual tasks.

5.Building a Strong Online Presence

Effective seo (search engine optimization) is a start line for a sturdy online presence. Search engine marketing guarantees that virtual content material ranks properly on search engine results pages, improving visibility and using organic visitors. Consistent branding across one-of-a-kind structures is equally critical. Visual factors, tone of voice, and messaging should align seamlessly, creating a recognizable and sincere logo identification.

6.Engaging with the Audience

Engaging the target market within the virtual space is dynamic and interactive. Creating interactive content, such as quizzes or polls on social media
(Example 1), captures target market attention and encourages participation. Building a community around a logo (Example 2) fosters loyalty and advocacy. Online communities, particularly on social media structures, offer an area for direct interplay, strengthening the bond among agencies and their target market.

7.Adapting to Technological Advances

Staying applicable in the speedy-paced virtual landscape entails adapting to technological advances. Integration of emerging technology like augmented fact (AR) and artificial intelligence (AI) (Example 1) can decorate consumer studies and set companies aside. Staying updated on technological trends allows corporations to explore modern answers and continue to be aggressive.

8.Mobile Optimization

Ensuring that websites, apps, and content material are easily reachable and user-pleasant on diverse devices is vital. A cellular-pleasant method (Example 1) complements person reports and aligns with changing consumer behaviors. Catering to the on-the-move nature of cutting-edge customers ensures that organizations stay related with their audience.

Conclusion, getting to know virtual systems is a persistent method that includes know-how the nuances of each platform, leveraging statistics for informed decision-making, constructing a constant online presence, engaging with the audience authentically, and adapting to technological advancements. It is an adventure of gaining knowledge of, adapting, and optimizing to meet the evolving demands of the digital age. Businesses that embody these principles position themselves for sustained success in the dynamic and competitive digital panorama.

Chapter 3i: Harnessing Social Media Dynamics

Harnessing social media dynamics is essential for corporations aiming to maximize their on-line presence, engage with their target market effectively, and construct a strong brand. Social media platforms provide a dynamic and ever-evolving area wherein agencies can connect to customers, exhibit their products or services, and foster significant relationships. Let's discover the key elements of harnessing social media dynamics for business success.

Understanding Social Media Dynamics

Social media systems, which however are no longer confined to Facebook, Instagram, Twitter, LinkedIn, and TikTok, each have their precise characteristics. Understanding the dynamics of every platform is crucial for corporations to tailor their content material and engagement techniques successfully.

1.Facebook: With its numerous person base, Facebook is a platform for connecting with friends, family, and groups. Businesses can create pages, percentage content material, and interact with their audience through posts, comments, and direct messages. Facebook's advertising functions also allow focused marketing to particular demographics.

2.Instagram: Known for its visible appeal, Instagram is a platform wherein corporations can exhibit products or services thru snap shots and short movies. The use of visually appealing content, along with splendid pics and attractive memories, is prime to capturing target audience interest on Instagram.

3. Twitter: Twitter's actual-time nature makes it appropriate for quick updates, information, and engaging in conversations. Businesses can share chew-sized content, participate in trending topics, and immediately speak with their audience through tweets and direct messages.

4. LinkedIn: Positioned as a professional networking platform, LinkedIn is ideal for B2B interactions, thought leadership, and profession-related content material. Businesses can percentage enterprise insights, hook up with professionals, and participate in organization discussions to establish authority in their niche.

5. TikTok: Known for its quick-form videos, TikTok is a platform in which companies can showcase creativity and authenticity. Engaging, enjoyable content frequently performs properly, and businesses can leverage trends and challenges to connect to a more youthful audience.

Crafting Engaging Content

1.Visual Appeal

 Visual content reigns perfect on social media. High-pleasant pictures, snap shots, and films seize attention. Businesses ought to spend money on developing visually appealing content that aligns with their brand identity.

2.Storytelling

Narratives resonate with audiences. Businesses can tell their brand tale, percentage at the back of-the-scenes glimpses, or highlight purchaser testimonials. Authentic storytelling builds connections and fosters a feel of network.

3.User-Generated Content

Encouraging customers to create content material associated with the brand may be powerful. User-generated content material now not most effective showcases authenticity however also involves the audience in the emblem narrative.

4. Interactive Elements
Polls, quizzes, and interactive features encourage audience participation. These factors now not most effectively improve engagement but additionally offer precious insights into client options.

Building a Community

1.Consistent Branding
Consistency in visible elements, tone of voice, and messaging throughout social media systems strengthens logo popularity. A cohesive logo identity builds acceptance

as true with and loyalty to most of the audience.

2.Responding to Feedback:

Social media is a -manner communication channel. Promptly responding to remarks, messages, and comments demonstrates a dedication to patron satisfaction and fosters a wonderful logo picture.

3.Creating Exclusive Groups

Some platforms provide the choice to create companies or communities. Businesses can leverage those capabilities to create spaces wherein clients can connect, percentage reviews, and have interaction immediately with the brand.

4.Live Sessions and Webinars:

Live video sessions allow businesses to connect with their audience in real-time.

Hosting webinars or Q&A sessions provides opportunities for direct engagement, answering questions, and showcasing expertise.

Strategic Use of Advertising:

1. **Targeted Ads**: Social media platforms offer robust advertising tools that allow businesses to target specific demographics, interests, and behaviors. This targeted approach ensures that ads reach the most relevant audience.

2. **Promoted Content**: Boosting posts or running sponsored content campaigns increases visibility. Promoted content can be used to highlight special offers, new products, or important announcements.

3. **Adaptation to Trends**: Staying updated on social media trends is

crucial. Businesses can leverage popular hashtags, challenges, or trends to amplify their reach and stay in tune with the current social media landscape.

Analyzing Performance Metrics:

1. **Key Performance Indicators (KPIs):** Businesses should identify relevant KPIs to measure the success of their social media efforts. Metrics like engagement rates, click-through rates, and conversion rates provide valuable insights into performance.

2. **Social Media Analytics Tools**: Platforms often provide built-in analytics tools, and additional third-party tools are available for more in-depth analysis. Regularly reviewing analytics helps businesses understand what works and refine their strategies accordingly.

Adaptability and Innovation:

1. **Embracing New Features**:
Social media platforms frequently introduce new features. Being early adopters of these features showcases a brand's adaptability and can provide a competitive edge.

2. **Monitoring Industry Trends**:
Keeping an eye on trends within the industry and on social media platforms ensures that businesses stay relevant. This adaptability is crucial for maintaining audience interest and engagement.

Conclusion: In the dynamic world of social media, businesses must actively harness the ever-evolving dynamics to build a strong online presence, engage their audience, and ultimately drive success. Crafting engaging content, building a community, strategically using advertising, analyzing performance metrics, and staying adaptable and innovative are essential components of a successful social media strategy. By understanding the unique dynamics of each platform and aligning strategies with business goals, businesses can navigate the social media landscape effectively and connect authentically with their audience.

Chapter 3ii: Unlocking the Power of SEO

Unlocking the electricity of search engine marketing (Search Engine Optimization) is akin to imparting your business with a sturdy online presence, ensuring clean discoverability by individuals looking for products or facts. Let's delve into the important elements of unleashing the ability of SEO on your enterprise success.

SEO as a Language: Search engine optimization serves because the language you operate to communicate with engines like google. When customers search for something online, search engine optimization enables your website to stand out as an applicable and sincere supply. It's now not pretty much impressing search engines like google and yahoo; it's about offering real price to the human beings searching.

Optimizing On-Page Elements

1. Keyword Integration: On-page optimization includes seamlessly integrating keywords into your content, headlines, and meta tags. These key phrases speak to the purpose of your pages to engines like google.

2. Engaging Content: Crafting engaging and treasured content is vital. Good content material no longer most effectively draws visitors but also signals to search engines like google that your internet site is a precious useful resource.

3. Meta Descriptions: Crafting compelling meta titles and outlines is like creating an invite. These snippets seem to seek outcomes, influencing whether users click for your site. Four.

User-Friendly Experience: Ensuring a consumer-friendly revel in your internet site is prime. A website that is simple to navigate and masses quick is more likely to rank better. Search engines respect websites that prioritize a high quality consumer revel in.

Building Quality Backlinks

1.External Links: Building connections with reliable websites on your enterprise, referred to as back-links, indicates to search engines that your content is worth recommending.

2. Internal Navigation: Internal navigation, or linking between pages on your personal website, helps customers explore greater of your content material and assists search engines in understanding the shape and relevance of your pages.

Technical search engine optimization

 1. Organized Website: Think of your internet site as a nicely-organized e book. Clear URLs, logical systems, and smooth navigation make it less complicated for serps to understand and index your content material.

2. Mobile-Friendly Design: With many customers surfing on their telephones, having a mobile-friendly internet site is vital. It guarantees an unbroken enjoyment, regardless of the tool they use. Three.

Site Speed Optimization: A speedy-loading internet site is a winner. Optimize your website online for speed by means of compressing pictures and minimizing unnecessary factors.

Content Strategy

 1.Comprehensive Content: Longer, comprehensive content material has a tendency to perform well in seeking effects. It gives you the possibility to thoroughly cover a topic and showcase your knowledge.

2.Evergreen Content: Crafting content material that stays relevant over the years, called evergreen content, ensures a regular go with the flow of visitors.

Local search engine marketing

1.Google My Business Optimization: For local corporations, optimizing your Google

My Business profile is like putting up a virtual signal. It includes correct information, patron evaluations, and relevant visuals.

2.Local Listings Consistency: Consistency throughout on line directories enhances your neighborhood search engine marketing. Accurate statistics tells search engines like google where your commercial enterprise is placed and boosts your visibility for local searches.

Analytics and Continuous Improvement

1.Google Analytics Insights: Tools like Google Analytics provide insights into how customers interact together with your internet site, assisting you make knowledgeable selections approximately what's running and what wishes improvement.

2. Routine search engine marketing Health Check: Regularly auditing your website for issues like broken hyperlinks or outdated content is like giving it a recurring fitness test. A healthful website is more likely to perform properly in search outcomes.

Adapting to Algorithm Updates

 1. Stay Informed: Staying informed about adjustments in search engine algorithms is critical. These updates impact how engines like google rank websites.

2.Quality Over Quantity: Quality content material and positive consumer reviews take precedence over previous SEO processes. Focus on providing actual value to your audience instead of counting on the amount.

 Conclusion, unlocking the energy of search engine marketing entails talking the language of serps, creating precious content material, building relationships on-line, and adapting to the ever-evolving virtual landscape. By incorporating these principles into your on-line approach, your business can advantage visibility, appeal to the right target market, and set up a strong online presence. SEO is not pretty much getting observed; it is about becoming a relied on and applicable supply inside the substantial virtual realm.

Chapter 4: Crafting Compelling Content

Crafting compelling content material is an art and science that goes past mere words on a web page. It involves know-how your target audience, placing clear goals, utilizing storytelling techniques, enhancing visible appeal, engaging with your audience efficiently, and measuring impact for continuous improvement.

Understanding Your Audience

Understanding your target market is foundational. Develop targeted target market personas – representations of your ideal clients. Consider demographics, interests, pain factors, and options. Empathize with your target market to create content material that addresses their demanding situations and dreams.

Defining Clear Objectives

Clearly define the purpose of your content. Align your targets with the favored final results and make certain consistency together with your emblem values. Each piece of content material must have a distinct motive to manual its advent and resonate together with your target market.

Crafting Engaging Headlines

Craft headlines that seize interest, evoke curiosity, or promise value. Use compelling language to trap readers or visitors to explore further. A well-crafted name sets the tone for the complete piece of content.

Storytelling Techniques

Organize your content with a logical and attractive glide. Infuse human factors into your content, inclusive of personal anecdotes or success tales. Storytelling captivates the target audience, making the content material extra memorable and relatable.

Visual Appeal

Visual factors beautify content material enchantment. Use wonderful photographs, photos, and videos that align along with your brand. Maintain regular visual branding to enhance brand reputation and make stronger the overall impact of your content material.

Engagement Strategies

Encourage target market interaction through polls, quizzes, or surveys. Clearly outline the preferred motion you need your target audience to take with a compelling call to movement. Interactive content and a robust CTA manual your target audience towards significant engagement.

Diverse Content Formats

Recognize that your target audience consumes content in numerous approaches. Offer a mix of formats consisting of written articles, movies, podcasts, and infographics. Repurpose a hit content into exclusive formats to maximize its fee and reach.

Audience Interaction

Actively reply to remarks, messages, and remarks. Engage along with your target audience in actual-time, fostering a feel of community. Encourage consumer-generated content material to offer various perspectives and exhibit proper studies.

Measuring Impact and Iterating

Utilize analytics gear to degree the overall performance of your content. Track metrics consisting of engagement prices, click-thru charges, and social shares. Embrace an attitude of non-stop improvement based on analytics and feedback for an applicable and effective content strategy through the years. In conclusion, crafting compelling content material involves a holistic technique that considers your target market, targets, storytelling, visuals, engagement, and non-stop development. By consistently delivering valuable and attractive content material, you not most effectively capture the eye of your target audience however additionally build lasting relationships and set up your logo as a depended on authority in your enterprise.

Chapter 4i: Storytelling in the Digital Age

Storytelling inside the digital age is a dynamic and effective tool for brands looking to connect to their audience on a deeper level. As conventional advertising evolves, narratives end up key in growing memorable, genuine, and engaging reviews. Let's explore how storytelling has evolved inside the digital landscape and the strategies that organizations can rent to craft compelling narratives that resonate with their target market.

The Evolution of Storytelling

 In the virtual age, storytelling has transitioned from conventional mediums like print and tv to a multi-platform experience. Digital structures such as social media, blogs, podcasts, and video content material have grown to be the brand new storytellers. Brands now have the possibility to create immersive narratives that spread across diverse channels, obtaining an international target audience immediately.

The Power of Visual Storytelling

Visual elements play an important position in digital storytelling. Platforms like Instagram, Pinterest, and TikTok thrive on visually attractive content. High-quality snapshots, videos, and infographics have the ability to carry a brand's tale succinctly and leave a lasting impact. Visuals not only seize interest but also evoke feelings, creating an extra profound reference to the target market.

Interactive Narratives

Digital storytelling goes beyond one-way conversation. Interactive elements inclusive of polls, quizzes, and augmented reality studies permit the audience to participate inside the narrative. Brands can have interaction with their target audience with the aid of permitting them to steer the storyline, making the experience greater personalized and noteworthy.

Transparency and Authenticity

In the virtual age, customers value transparency and authenticity. Authentic storytelling includes being true, sharing behind-the-scenes glimpses, and showcasing real stories. Social media systems provide a street for brands to humanize their narrative, fostering trust and loyalty among clients who recognize honesty.

User-Generated Content (UGC)

Digital storytelling encourages user participation through UGC. Encouraging clients to share their reports and stories related to the brand creates a network experience. UGC not most effectively diversifies the narrative but additionally leverages the collective creativity of the target audience, making them energetic participants to the emblem's story.

Storytelling Across Platforms

Different virtual platforms require tailored storytelling approaches. Twitter's concise format demands succinct and impactful storytelling, while structures like YouTube offer space for more in-depth and immersive narratives. Brands should adapt their storytelling strategies to healthy the nuances of each platform, ensuring most effect.

Incorporating Data into Narratives

Data-pushed storytelling is a rising trend inside the virtual panorama. Brands can use statistics to support their narratives, imparting proof and insights that resonate with the audience. Infographics, facts visualizations, and case studies make contributions to a greater compelling and persuasive digital narrative.

Embracing Transmedia Storytelling

Transmedia storytelling entails distributing a narrative across more than one structure, growing a cohesive and interconnected experience. Brands can weave a tale that spans social media, blogs, podcasts, and different channels, ensuring an unbroken and engaging journey for the audience. Each platform contributes a completely unique detail to the overarching narrative.

Emotional Resonance

Emotional storytelling remains an undying detail inside the virtual age. Brands that evoke feelings in their narratives hook up with their audience on a deeper level. Whether it's pleasure, empathy, or inspiration, eliciting emotional responses enhances the memorability of the brand's story.

Measuring Impact and Iterating

Digital storytelling permits brands to measure the impact of their narratives in real-time. Analytics equipment provides insights into audience engagement, click on-thru rates, and social shares. Brands can use these records to iterate and refine their storytelling techniques, making sure ongoing relevance and effectiveness.

Challenges and Opportunities

While digital storytelling affords big possibilities, it also comes with challenges.

The digital landscape is crowded, making it crucial for brands to stand out. Cutting through the noise requires creativity, authenticity, and a deep knowledge of the target audience.

Conclusion

Storytelling in the digital age is a powerful approach for brands to connect with their target audience in significant methods. Leveraging visible factors, embracing transparency, encouraging consumer participation, and adapting storytelling strategies to different platforms are crucial techniques. By incorporating statistics, embracing transmedia storytelling, and evoking emotional resonance, manufacturers can create compelling narratives that leave a long-lasting impact. The virtual landscape provides a dynamic canvas for manufacturers to weave narratives that no longer simplest capture attention but additionally build lasting relationships with their audience.

Chapter 4 ii: Visuals and Multimedia Impact

Visuals and multimedia factors play a pivotal role in the virtual panorama, shaping how information is consumed and studies are created. From fascinating pix to engaging motion pictures, the effect of visuals is simple in shooting attention, conveying messages, and fostering a deeper reference to the audience. Let's discover the importance of visuals and multimedia in the digital realm and the strategies that businesses can hire to harness their full effect.

The Power of Visual Communication

Visuals have a completely unique ability to convey complex facts quickly and efficiently. In a global wherein attention spans are shrinking, compelling visuals can seize attention inside seconds, making them an invaluable device for manufacturers aiming to communicate their message efficiently.

Immediate Impact

Humans are incredibly visible beings, processing pictures a whole lot faster than textual content. A well-crafted visual can deliver emotions, tell a story, or talk about a concept immediately. This instant impact is particularly vital within the rapid-paced digital environment, where customers scroll through large amounts of content day by day.

Enhancing Brand Identity

Consistent visual elements, which include logos, color schemes, and imagery, contribute to brand identification. When customers come upon those visuals throughout numerous systems, they increase a visual connection with the logo. This visible consistency facilitates in emblem reputation and fosters a feel of acceptance as true with and familiarity.

Creating Memorable Experiences

Multimedia elements, which include motion pictures, animations, and interactive content, enhance the general consumer's enjoyment. They create a more immersive and noteworthy come-up with the logo. By leveraging multimedia, agencies can leave a lasting effect on their target market, growing the likelihood of emblems do not forget.

Social Media Dominance

Visual content material dominates social media systems. Posts with photos or films tend to acquire better engagement than text-best posts. Platforms like Instagram, Pinterest, and TikTok thrive on visually appealing content, emphasizing the importance of visuals in shaping social media narratives.

Effective Storytelling

Visuals are effective storytellers. They evoke feelings, deliver narratives, and make statistics more relatable. Whether via static photographs or dynamic movies, manufacturers can use visuals to inform compelling memories that resonate with their target market on a deeper level.

Search Engine Optimization (search engine optimization) Benefits

Search engines prioritize visible content material. Including images and films to your website now not only complements personal experience but also contributes to higher seek engine scores. Alt text, image descriptions, and relevant document names offer extra opportunities for search engine optimization optimization.

Strategies for Maximum Impact

1.High-Quality Imagery: Invest in splendid visuals that align along with your brand's aesthetic. Sharp, clean, and properly-composed snap shots convey professionalism and make contributions to an effective brand photo.

2.Consistent Branding: Maintain visual consistency across all structures. Use a constant color palette, fonts, and layout elements to reinforce your logo identity. Consistency builds brand popularity and acceptance as true.

3.Interactive Content: Incorporate interactive factors consisting of polls, quizzes, and clickable pics. Interactive content material encourages consumer engagement, imparting a greater participatory and memorable enjoyment.

4.Video Storytelling: Leverage the energy of video to inform your emblem tale. Whether through product demonstrations, behind-the-scenes glimpses, or patron testimonials, motion pictures can bring feelings and messages efficiently.

5.Infographics for Information: Complex facts may be made digestible through infographics. Create visually attractive infographics to break down statistics, tactics, or ideas into without difficulty comprehensible visual factors.

6.User-Generated Content (UGC): Encourage your target audience to create and proportion visual content material related to your logo. UGC not simplest diversifies your content however additionally builds a feel of community around your brand.

7. Adapt to Platform Nuances: Tailor your visible content for every platform. Understand the nuances of structures like Instagram, Facebook, Twitter, and LinkedIn to optimize your visuals for optimum effect.

8.Mobile Optimization: Given the prevalence of mobile browsing, ensure that your visuals are optimized for various gadgets. Responsive design ensures a unbroken visible revel in throughout smartphones, capsules, and desktops.

Challenges and Considerations

While visuals and multimedia elements offer several advantages, corporations must bear in mind capability demanding situations:

1.Accessibility: Ensure that visuals are accessible to all customers, together with those with visual impairments. Use descriptive alt textual content and provide alternative content material wherein important.

2.Loading Speed: High-decision visuals can affect internet site loading pace. Optimize photographs and motion pictures to maintain speedy load times, preventing person frustration.

3.Cultural Sensitivity: Visuals need to be culturally sensitive and inclusive. Consider numerous representations in your visuals to resonate with a broader audience.

Conclusion: Visuals and multimedia elements are integral in the virtual era, influencing how manufacturers communicate, interact, and leave a lasting impact on their target audience. By strategically incorporating tremendous visuals, interactive content material, and platform-specific strategies, businesses can harness the overall effect of visuals to create compelling and memorable digital studies. As the virtual panorama continues to adapt, visual storytelling remains a dynamic and important aspect of successful on-line engagement.

Chapter 5: Analytics and Optimization

Unveiling the Power of Analytics and Optimization in Modern Marketing

In the short-paced realm of modern advertising, the wedding of analytics and optimization has emerged as a linchpin for achievement. As corporations navigate the virtual panorama and client options evolve, leveraging statistics-pushed insights and refining strategies via optimization have turned out to be imperative. This article explores the multifaceted function of analytics and optimization in modern-day advertising, unraveling how these twin forces power agencies towards enhanced overall performance, multiplied ROI, and a competitive part.

1. The Landscape of Modern Marketing: Modern advertising is a dynamic area in which virtual channels, social media, and an ever-related purchaser form the gambling subject. In this panorama, analytics serves as the compass, supplying marketers with the capacity to navigate the complexities and uncertainties. Through sophisticated tools and technologies, corporations can gain a granular know-how of consumer behavior, marketplace tendencies, and the overall performance of diverse marketing channels.

2. The Crucial Role of Analytics:Analytics in contemporary marketing is going past mere facts collection. It involves the systematic analysis of considerable datasets to extract actionable insights. Understanding client conduct is paramount, and analytics gives a panoramic view of customer interactions with products, offerings, and marketing content. By dissecting this information, marketers can discover patterns, alternatives, and ache points, enabling them to tailor techniques that resonate with their target market.

3. Personalization and Targeted Campaigns: One of the key results of analytics in contemporary advertising is the potential to customize campaigns. Armed with insights into personal possibilities and behaviors, entrepreneurs can craft targeted and customized messages. Whether through electronic mail campaigns, social media marketing, or internet site content material, personalization complements purchaser engagement, fosters emblem loyalty, and contributes to an extra significant purchaser revel in.

4. Real-Time Adaptability: In the dynamic panorama of modern marketing, agility is non-negotiable. Analytics empowers entrepreneurs with actual-time information, letting them adapt fast to converting marketplace conditions. By tracking real-time metrics, corporations could make informed choices on-the-fly, optimizing campaigns, reallocating budgets, and pivoting strategies based on the brand new insights. This adaptability is a cornerstone for staying in advance in a competitive marketplace.

5. Optimization Strategies in Action: Analytics affords the basis, however it is through optimization that marketing techniques come to lifestyles. Once insights are gleaned, the optimization system kicks in, refining and pleasant-tuning numerous elements of advertising efforts. For instance, if analytics reveal a drop in conversion prices for a selected ad campaign, optimization might also involve tweaking ad creatives, adjusting concentrated on parameters, or refining the decision-to-movement to better resonate with the target audience.

6. Multichannel Marketing Optimization: Modern advertising regularly involves achieving customers across a couple of channels – social media, e-mail, serps, and more. Optimization in this context calls for a holistic technique. By analyzing overall performance metrics throughout channels, agencies can allocate sources successfully, focusing on channels that supply the very best ROI. This move-channel optimization guarantees a cohesive and impactful advertising approach that maximizes attainment and engagement.

7. Customer Journey Mapping and Optimization: Understanding the consumer journey is a cornerstone of present day advertising fulfillment. Analytics helps the mapping of client touchpoints and interactions, revealing the stages of the buying manner. Optimization efforts then revolve round streamlining this journey, getting rid of friction factors, and ensuring a seamless revel in. This consumer-centric optimization now not simplest enhances patron delight however also increases the probability of conversions.

8. A/B Testing and Continuous Improvement: Optimization is an iterative system, and A/B checking out is a powerful tool inside this framework. Marketers can test with different variations of ads, landing pages, or email campaigns and use analytics to measure their impact. Through continuous A/B testing, agencies can discover what resonates excellently with their audience, leading to ongoing enhancements and expanded effectiveness of advertising efforts.

Conclusion: In the panorama of current advertising, analytics and optimization aren't mere equipment but strategic imperatives. The symbiotic dating between those forces empowers businesses to navigate the complexities of the digital age, turning in centered, personalized, and impactful advertising and marketing campaigns. As generation advances and client expectations evolve, embracing analytics and optimization will become no longer only a competitive benefit however a need for those searching for to thrive and excel within the ever-evolving world of current advertising.

Chapter 5i: Measuring Campaign Effectiveness

Measuring campaign effectiveness in modern advertising is a multifaceted method that goes beyond conventional metrics. In an era ruled via digital channels, statistics analytics, and a dynamic client landscape, companies must appoint a comprehensive approach to evaluate the success in their advertising campaigns. Let's explore key strategies and metrics for measuring marketing campaign effectiveness inside the contemporary advertising panorama.

Defining Success Objectives:

Before diving into metrics, it is crucial to establish clear campaign objectives. Whether aiming to increase logo focus, drive website site visitors, generate leads, or boost income, defining precise, measurable, practicable, relevant, and time-certain (SMART) goals offers a basis for effective size.

Multi-Channel Attribution:

Modern advertising often involves a mixture of channels, from social media and e-mail to content material marketing and paid advertising and marketing. Multi-channel attribution fashions assist characteristic conversions to the diverse touchpoints in a customer's journey. Understanding how specific channels make a contribution to conversions gives insights into the general impact of the campaign.

Conversion Tracking:

Tracking conversions is essential to measuring marketing campaign fulfillment. Whether a conversion is described as a buy, shape submission, or every other desired movement, putting in place strong tracking mechanisms, which include pixels and tags, allows businesses to attribute specific results to their advertising efforts correctly.

Customer Lifetime Value (CLV):

Focusing on obtaining new customers is essential, however understanding the long-time period fee of received customers affords a greater complete view. CLV measures the entire revenue a business can anticipate from a consumer at some stage in their relationship. This metric helps evaluate the impact of marketing campaigns on consumer retention and loyalty.

Return on Investment (ROI):

ROI is a fundamental metric for determining the profitability of an advertising campaign. It compares the campaign's profits towards its prices, presenting a clean picture of the return generated. Calculating ROI entails subtracting the campaign expenses from the sales generated and dividing the result with the aid of the charges.

Brand Metrics:

For campaigns centered on brand recognition and notion, monitoring logo metrics is crucial. Metrics like emblem mentions, sentiment analysis, and logo visibility can gauge how the marketing campaign affects emblem perception of some of the target market.

Social Media Engagement:

In a technology in which social media is a dominant advertising channel, monitoring engagement metrics is vital. Metrics such as likes, stocks, feedback, and click-via costs on social media systems offer insights into audience interaction and the effectiveness of content material.

Website Analytics:

Examining internet site analytics gives treasured data on person behavior. Metrics like website site visitors, jump costs, time spent on website online, and web page perspectives can indicate the marketing campaign's impact on riding visitors and preserving them engaged.

Customer Surveys and Feedback:

Direct comments from customers is worthwhile. Implementing surveys and amassing qualitative remarks can offer insights into the client experience, delight levels, and perceptions fashioned by means of the marketing campaign.

Email Marketing Metrics:

For campaigns that leverage e-mail marketing, tracking metrics which include open prices, click-through fees, conversion fees, and subscriber growth provides a complete view of electronic mail campaign effectiveness. A/B checking out can assist optimize email content material for higher overall performance.

Customer Journey Analysis:

Understanding the patron's adventure from cognizance to conversion is vital. Analyzing touchpoints and the effectiveness of every degree in guiding customers through the sales funnel allows refine advertising strategies for destiny campaigns.

Adapting to Real-Time Analytics:

Modern marketing operates in actual-time, and campaigns want to evolve quickly to convert dynamics. Utilizing actual-time analytics lets entrepreneurs monitor marketing campaign overall performance as it unfolds, permitting well timed changes and optimizations for higher consequences.

Challenges and Considerations:

Despite the wealth of metrics available, challenges exist in interpreting statistics appropriately. Attribution modeling, distinguishing between causation and correlation, and accounting for external elements affecting overall performance are ongoing issues inside the size procedure.

Conclusion

Measuring marketing campaign effectiveness in cutting-edge advertising calls for a holistic technique that incorporates a diverse set of metrics aligned with marketing campaign goals. From conversion monitoring and multi-channel attribution to ROI analysis and patron surveys, businesses must leverage a mixture of quantitative and qualitative facts to gain a comprehensive know-how of their advertising and marketing effect. In a landscape wherein consumer conduct evolves unexpectedly, adapting to real-time analytics and constantly refining strategies based totally on insights are important for accomplishing sustained achievement in modern-day advertising and marketing campaigns.

Chapter 5 ii: Iterative Strategies for Success

Iterative techniques are vital in navigating the ever-evolving landscape of present day advertising. In an environment fashioned by using dynamic customer behaviors, technological improvements, and evolving developments, organizations should undertake an iterative approach to live adaptable, applicable, and a hit. Let's delve into key iterative techniques that may propel fulfillment in present day marketing.

Continuous Data Analysis

Iterative strategies start with a commitment to continuous records analysis. Regularly tracking key overall performance indicators (KPIs), client behavior, and market trends presents insights that drive knowledgeable choice-making. Utilizing superior analytics gear permits businesses to perceive styles, options, and regions for improvement, laying the muse for iterative adjustments.

Agile Marketing Practices:

Embracing agile advertising and marketing practices is critical to iterative achievement. Agile methodologies prioritize flexibility, collaboration, and responsiveness. Breaking down advertising initiatives into smaller, possible tasks, known as sprints, allows teams to quickly adapt to changing occasions and comprise learnings from ongoing campaigns.

A/B Testing and Experimentation

A/B testing involves comparing versions of a marketing detail to determine which performs higher. Whether trying out electronic mail situation strains, ad creatives, or internet site designs, experimentation presents treasured insights into what resonates with the target audience. Iteratively refining based on A/B testing results guarantees continuous optimization for advanced outcomes.

Dynamic Content Optimization

Personalization is a cornerstone of contemporary advertising and marketing, and dynamic content material optimization takes personalization to the next stage. By dynamically adjusting content material based totally on consumer behavior, preferences, or demographics, organizations can tailor their messaging in actual-time. This iterative technique complements relevance, engagement, and conversion rates.

Customer Feedback Integration:

Customers are a precious source of insights. Integrating consumer feedback into advertising and marketing strategies allows organizations to apprehend their audience's choices, expectations, and pain points. Surveys, critiques, and social media interactions offer rich qualitative statistics that can tell iterative upgrades in products, services, and marketing messaging.

Iterative search engine optimization Strategies

Search engine algorithms evolve, and businesses have to iterate their search engine optimization techniques to remain seen. Regularly auditing and updating content material, optimizing for brand spanking new keywords, and adapting to algorithm modifications are critical iterative steps. Staying knowledgeable about search engine optimization trends ensures that organizations maintain or enhance their search engine rankings.

Responsive Social Media Strategies

Social media is a dynamic space where trends, algorithms, and personal behaviors evolve unexpectedly. Iterative social media techniques contain adapting content material, posting schedules, and engagement strategies primarily based on real-time analytics. Staying agile on social structures guarantees that businesses correctly connect with their audience and capitalize on rising possibilities.

Leveraging Marketing Automation

 Marketing automation equipment streamline repetitive obligations, allowing entrepreneurs to recognize strategy and creativity. Iterative refinement of automation workflows guarantees that groups live efficiently and responsive. Regularly reviewing and optimizing automation sequences primarily based on overall performance facts prevents stagnation and complements campaign effectiveness.

User Experience (UX) Iterations

The user enjoyment is pivotal in current advertising. Businesses must iteratively refine their website, app, or virtual platform based totally on user comments and conduct. Conducting usability testing, studying heatmaps, and in search of enter from real customers make a contribution to ongoing enhancements that enhance the general consumer experience.

Adapting to Emerging Technologies

Iterative techniques contain staying abreast of rising technology and incorporating them strategically. Whether it is augmented reality, voice search optimization, or chatbots, adopting and iteratively refining generation-driven advertising and marketing initiatives positions companies at the vanguard of innovation.

Incorporating Sustainability Initiatives

Sustainability and social duty are more and more critical elements for clients. Iteratively integrating and communicating sustainability tasks aligns with evolving consumer values. Regularly assessing the impact of sustainability messaging and adapting techniques guarantees authenticity and relevance.

Iterative Content Marketing

Content is a dynamic pressure in current advertising and marketing. Iterative content material techniques contain often auditing content overall performance, updating previous cloth, and experimenting with new codecs. Monitoring target market engagement metrics and adapting content material based totally on converting options guarantees sustained impact.

Challenges and Considerations

While iterative strategies are effective, demanding situations exist. Balancing the need for generation with preserving a cohesive emblem identity, averting over-reliance on short-term statistics fluctuations, and making sure alignment with lengthy-term dreams are considerations inside the iterative process.

Conclusion

Iterative strategies shape the backbone of successful modern-day marketing. Through continuous information evaluation, agile practices, A/B checking out, and responsive variations to rising trends, corporations can navigate the dynamic landscape successfully. Embracing an iterative attitude fosters a culture of innovation, responsiveness, and perceptual development, making sure that advertising and marketing techniques remain effective, applicable, and resilient inside the face of consistent trade.

Conclusion

Effortless Marketing Mastery: Strategies for the Modern Business presents a comprehensive exploration of contemporary marketing approaches, offering valuable insights and actionable strategies for businesses navigating the dynamic landscape of today's marketplace. Throughout the book, the author emphasizes the importance of adapting to changing consumer behaviors, technological advancements, and emerging trends in order to achieve marketing mastery with minimal effort. As we conclude our journey through the pages of this insightful guide, several key takeaways emerge.

One of the central themes of the book is the notion that effective marketing doesn't have to be arduous; rather, it can be a streamlined and efficient process. The author argues that businesses can achieve success by understanding their target audience, leveraging digital tools, and optimizing their marketing efforts. By embracing a mindset of simplicity and focusing on the most impactful strategies, organizations can position themselves for sustained growth in the modern business landscape.

The book delves into the power of data-driven decision-making, highlighting the significance of analytics in shaping successful marketing campaigns. Through the lens of case studies and real-world examples, readers gain an appreciation for the role of data in identifying consumer preferences, measuring campaign performance, and refining strategies for maximum impact. This data-centric approach is presented as a key element of effortless marketing mastery, enabling businesses to make informed decisions and adapt swiftly to market changes.

Furthermore, the author emphasizes the importance of building a strong online presence and leveraging digital channels to connect with audiences. The book provides actionable insights into creating compelling content, optimizing websites for search engines, and utilizing social media platforms effectively. In the conclusion, it becomes evident that a strategic and well-executed online presence is a cornerstone of modern marketing success, allowing businesses to reach and engage with their target audience in meaningful ways.

The concept of automation emerges as another critical aspect of effortless marketing mastery. The book argues that businesses can streamline repetitive tasks, enhance efficiency, and ensure consistent messaging through the judicious use of marketing automation tools. By automating certain processes, organizations can free up valuable time and resources, allowing them to focus on strategic planning and creative endeavors that contribute to long-term success.

Throughout the chapters, the author underlines the importance of adaptability in the face of evolving market trends. Effortless marketing mastery is portrayed as a continuous journey of learning and adjustment, with businesses encouraged to stay agile and responsive to emerging opportunities and challenges. The conclusion reinforces the idea that a mindset of adaptability is crucial for sustained success in the ever-changing business landscape.

As we reflect on the book's insights, it becomes clear that collaboration and relationship-building are integral components of effortless marketing mastery. The author advocates for cultivating strong connections with customers, influencers, and other businesses. By fostering meaningful relationships, organizations can amplify their reach, build trust, and create a positive brand image. The conclusion reinforces the idea that collaboration is not only beneficial for individual campaigns but is a long-term strategy for building a resilient and successful business.

In the final chapters, the book explores the ethical dimensions of marketing, emphasizing the importance of transparency, authenticity, and social responsibility. Effortless marketing mastery, according to the author, goes hand in hand with ethical practices that resonate with today's conscious consumers. The conclusion encourages businesses to embrace ethical considerations as a fundamental aspect of their marketing strategies, recognizing that a positive reputation and ethical behavior contribute significantly to long-term success.

In summary, Effortless Marketing Mastery: Strategies for the Modern Business provides a holistic perspective on contemporary marketing, guiding readers through the intricacies of digital landscapes, data-driven decision-making, automation, adaptability, collaboration, and ethical considerations. The book challenges the notion that effective marketing requires excessive effort and complex strategies, presenting a compelling case for simplicity and efficiency in achieving marketing mastery. As we conclude our exploration of this insightful guide, it is clear that businesses willing to embrace the principles outlined within will be well-positioned to navigate the challenges of the modern business environment and achieve sustained success with ease.

Review Page

Effortless Marketing Mastery is a compelling guide that navigates the complex landscape of contemporary marketing with finesse and practicality. Authored by a marketing expert [Author's Name], the book offers a refreshing perspective on crafting and implementing effective marketing strategies without overwhelming complexity.

The strength of this book lies in its ability to demystify marketing concepts, making them accessible to both seasoned professionals and newcomers in the business world. [Author's Name] employs a conversational tone that engages the reader, creating an enjoyable reading experience while delivering invaluable insights.

One of the standout features of Effortless Marketing Mastery is its emphasis on adaptability. In a rapidly evolving business environment, the author advocates for flexible strategies that can withstand the test of time. The book provides a roadmap for staying current with marketing trends and technologies, ensuring that readers are well-equipped to tackle the challenges of the modern marketplace.

The practical examples and case studies scattered throughout the book serve as real-world illustrations of the strategies presented. This hands-on approach helps readers connect theoretical concepts to practical applications, fostering a deeper understanding of the marketing principles at play.

Effortless Marketing Mastery also places a strong focus on leveraging digital tools and platforms. From social media marketing to search engine optimization, the book provides actionable advice on harnessing the power of the digital landscape to enhance brand visibility and engagement.

While the title may suggest an effortless approach, the book doesn't shy away from the reality that successful marketing requires dedication and strategic thinking. It encourages readers to embrace a mindset of continuous improvement and to view challenges as opportunities for growth.

In conclusion, Effortless Marketing Mastery stands out as a valuable resource for anyone looking to master the art of marketing in the modern business landscape. With its practical insights, engaging writing style, and emphasis on adaptability, this book is a must-read for entrepreneurs, marketers, and business professionals seeking to elevate their marketing game in today's competitive environment.